THE HUMAN BODY IN 3D

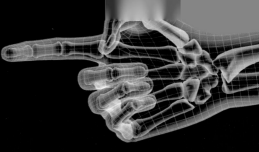

THE BRAIN AND SPINAL CORD IN 3D

rosen publishing's
rosen central®

JACK BECKER AND
CHRIS HAYHURST

Published in 2016 by The Rosen Publishing Group, Inc.
29 East 21st Street, New York, NY 10010

Copyright © 2016 by The Rosen Publishing Group, Inc.

First Edition

Library of Congress Cataloging-in-Publication Data

Becker, Jack.
The brain and spinal cord in 3D / Jack Becker and Chris Hayhurst.—First edition.
    pages cm.—(The human body in 3D)
Audience: Grades 5 to 8.
Includes bibliographical references and index.
ISBN 978-1-4994-3581-8 (library bound) — ISBN 978-1-4994-3583-2 (pbk.) —
ISBN 978-1-4994-3584-9 (6-pack)
1. Central nervous system—Juvenile literature. I. Hayhurst, Chris. II. Title.
QP361.5.B43 2016
612.8'2--dc23
                                                                          2015000239

Manufactured in the United States of America

CONTENTS

INTRODUCTION

The human body is an amazing creation. It is an intricate network of nerves, veins, muscles, bones, and organs too complex for most to understand. Anyone who has had to memorize all the bones of the body for a biology class understands just how much there is to know. And that is just the tip of the iceberg! Indeed, it is one thing to be able to identify all the elements and yet another to understand how they all work.

And yet, when our bodies are working well, which is most of the time, we don't even notice how intricate they are. This is because our complex network of systems runs without any real effort from us. If a ball flies across the park directly in the path of your head, somehow you know, without thinking, to duck. Without worrying about it, your body inhales oxygen and exhales carbon dioxide. Your blood pumps through your brain and to your organs regardless of whether you know it needs to be done.

This is all possible thanks to the brain and spinal cord. Everyone knows that the brain is responsible for how smart you are and that the spinal cord holds you up, but there is much more to both of them. Together they form the central nervous system (CNS), which is involved in everything we do. The CNS controls all the things we do without thinking, such as swallowing, blinking, breathing and converting food into fuel. It also is involved in the way we think, learn, and express emotion.

Located at the top of your body, beneath the protection of your skull, the brain transmits and receives messages to and from the rest of your body. These messages tell the brain when the body should feel pain (although the brain itself has no pain receptors and cannot feel pain) or hunger, for example. The brain also contains different regions that are responsible for thinking, learning and memory; emotion; balance and muscle control; and speech.

The spinal cord runs down the center of your body. It connects to the brain at the brain stem. The spinal cord is protected by the spinal column—which includes the vertebrae that allow you to stand upright—and is made up of countless bundles of nerves that transmit information between the brain and nerves throughout the rest of the body.

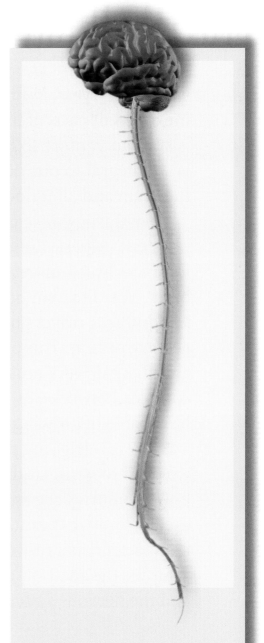

Together the brain and spinal cord form the central nervous system, one of two divisions of the body's nervous system.

Researchers are uncovering new information about the brain every year. While we now understand a great deal about the different parts of the brain and how it impacts the body, there is still much more to learn. This fascinating and complex organ is so integral to our daily lives that uncovering the mysteries of the brain and all it does is vital to modern medical science.

For instance, scientists who studied the brain of brilliant physicist Albert Einstein found that the regions responsible for math were more than 30 percent wider than the average brain. Was Einstein born this way? Researchers have noted that London taxi drivers have larger hippocampus regions than the average person. This part of the brain is responsible for memory, and these drivers must be able to remember London's vast and complex network of streets. This suggests the hippocampus may be capable of growing as more and more knowledge is gained.

These intriguing pieces of trivia illustrate how much further we need to go in studying the brain to determine, for example, how memories are stored and retrieved, why brains sleep and dream, and what exactly emotions are. These are questions that neuroscientists are working hard to explain. But for now, let's examine the anatomy and functions of the brain, the spinal cord, and the nervous system.

CHAPTER ONE

YOUR BODY'S MOST COMPLEX ORGAN

Weighing in at 3 pounds (1.3 kilograms) and taking the honor of being one of the most essential and complicated pieces of the human body, the human brain has been endlessly studied by medical professionals and scientists throughout history. Yet it remains very much a mystery. For as much as we know about this fascinating organ, we still have a long way to go in terms of understanding how it affects our behavior, our personalities, and our entire existence.

The human brain is an incredibly important piece of anatomical machinery. Your body would be completely useless without it. You couldn't read this book. Writing would be impossible. You'd have no memory, no thoughts, no emotions, and no way to breathe. You couldn't see, feel, sleep, eat, walk, talk, or log onto the Internet. You need your brain for absolutely everything you do.

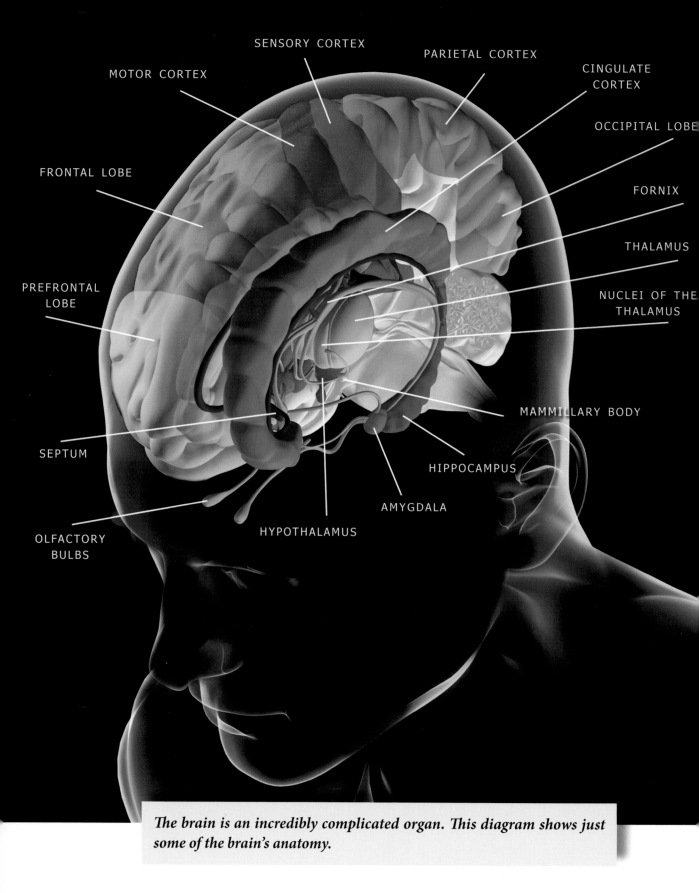

MOTOR CORTEX

SENSORY CORTEX

PARIETAL CORTEX

CINGULATE CORTEX

OCCIPITAL LOBE

FORNIX

THALAMUS

NUCLEI OF THE THALAMUS

FRONTAL LOBE

PREFRONTAL LOBE

SEPTUM

OLFACTORY BULBS

HYPOTHALAMUS

AMYGDALA

HIPPOCAMPUS

MAMMILLARY BODY

The brain is an incredibly complicated organ. This diagram shows just some of the brain's anatomy.

Were you to crack your skull wide open, pull your brain out, and cradle it in your hands, first off, you'd be dead. But if, for educational purposes only, you did survive, you'd see a slimy, lumpy, pinkish-gray mass of mush. It would look a lot like a gray walnut, only much bigger, far heavier, and a lot less appetizing.

FIVE PROTECTIVE LAYERS

Since it's such a vital organ, it should come as no surprise that the brain is guarded from harm by no less than five protective layers. The first and outermost layer is the skull. The skull surrounds the brain like a permanent and perfectly fitted bicycle helmet. It's hard, sturdy, and a great first defense against everyday bangs and bumps. The skull is the brain's brick wall—its main coat of armor, so to speak.

The brain's next three layers of protection are collectively known as meninges. The meninges are separate sheets of body tissue that stack up one on top of the other. The outer strip, a tough membrane attached to the inside of the skull, is known as the dura mater (*dura mater* means "tough mother" in Latin). Just beneath that is the middle meningeal layer, called the arachnoid. Finally, below the arachnoid—and separated from it by a narrow gap known as the subarachnoid space—is the third meningeal layer, the pia mater, which clings to the brain and all its numerous pits (sulci) and folds (gyri) like plastic

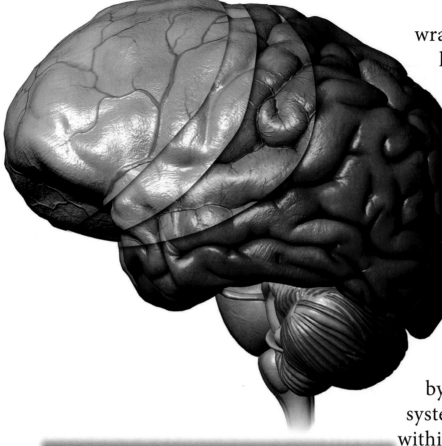

Three of the human brain's five protective layers are together known as meninges.

wrap on a chunk of raw hamburger.

Last among the brain's physical protectors, but certainly not least, is a clear, water-like substance known as cerebral spinal fluid, or CSF. CSF is produced by the brain's vascular system and circulates within the subarachnoid space. It acts like a liquid cushion between the brain and the skull.

THE BRAIN'S THREE MAJOR SECTIONS

Beneath the meningeal layers is the real meat of the brain. There are three main parts: the cerebrum, the cerebellum, and the brain stem.

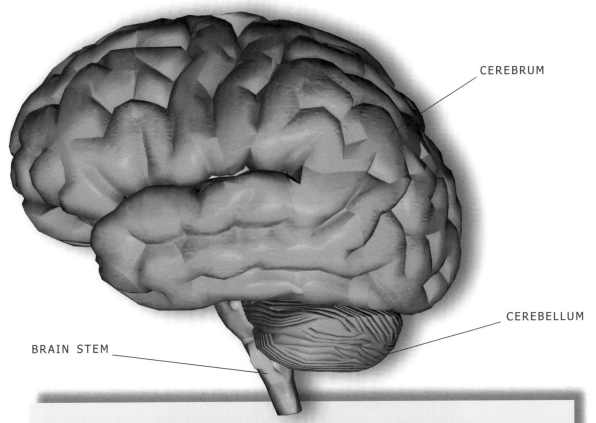

CEREBRUM

CEREBELLUM

BRAIN STEM

The cerebrum is responsible for thinking, sensing, emotion, and consciousness. Balance and fine muscle movement are coordinated in the cerebellum. The brain stem is a conductor for information.

The cerebrum is the brain's largest component, accounting for most of its weight and nearly three-fourths of its volume. It forms the top of the brain and is the control center for thoughts, feelings, sensations, and voluntary actions. The hills and valleys of the cerebrum are covered by a layer of tissue called the cerebral cortex, and the cerebrum is physically divided into two halves by a deep, canyon-like groove called the longitudinal fissure. The left side of the split is known as the left cerebral hemisphere. The right half is called the right cerebral hemisphere.

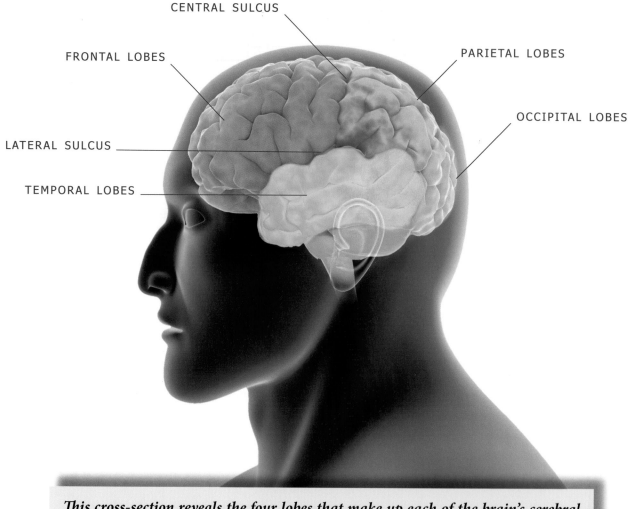

CENTRAL SULCUS

FRONTAL LOBES

PARIETAL LOBES

OCCIPITAL LOBES

LATERAL SULCUS

TEMPORAL LOBES

This cross-section reveals the four lobes that make up each of the brain's cerebral hemispheres.

Each hemisphere consists of four rounded cerebral lobes, or regions. The lobes are named after the particular skull bones that protect them and, like the cerebral hemispheres, are separated by fissures. The frontal lobes are located in the front, or ventral portion, of each hemisphere. Parietal lobes are medial—that is, they're near the middle. Occipital lobes are dorsal, or in the back; and temporal lobes are lateral and inferior, along the bottom sides. The central sulcus (a deep fissure) divides the frontal and parietal lobes, while the lateral sulcus separates the temporal lobe from the parietal and frontal lobes.

In order for the two hemispheres to function efficiently with one another, they must be connected, and that job goes to the corpus callosum. The corpus callosum is an arching network of fibers that bridges the hemispheres from its location just above the brain stem. By linking the hemispheres together, it allows them to communicate and cooperate

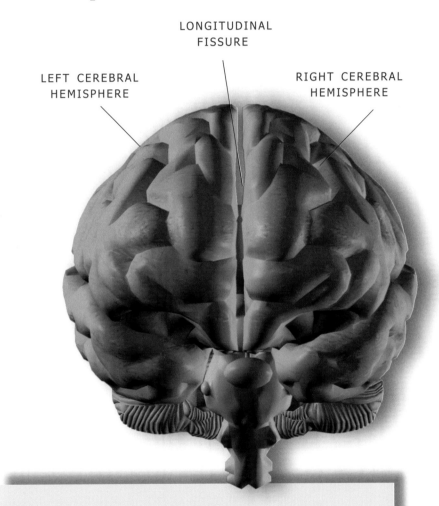

LONGITUDINAL FISSURE

LEFT CEREBRAL HEMISPHERE

RIGHT CEREBRAL HEMISPHERE

This view from above shows how the longitudinal fissure that runs down the middle of the brain separates the two hemispheres of the cerebral cortex.

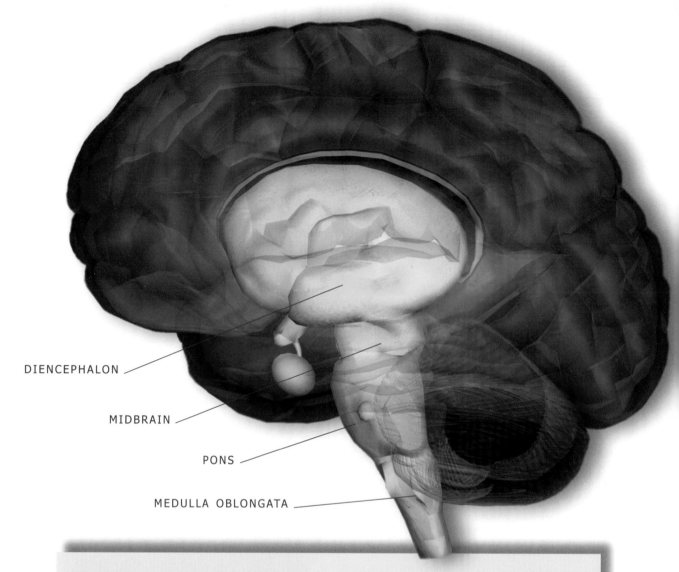

DIENCEPHALON

MIDBRAIN

PONS

MEDULLA OBLONGATA

The brain stem is one of the major sections of the brain. The four parts that make up the brain stem are the diencephalon, midbrain, pons, and medulla oblongata.

with each other. So when information is received by or sent from one hemisphere, the other hemisphere knows all about it.

A second major brain part lies inferior and dorsal to the cerebrum's occipital lobe and is known as the cerebellum.

"Cerebellum" comes from the Latin word for "little brain," and that's exactly what it is—a miniature version of the cerebrum, which most people think of as "the brain." The cerebellum is responsible for unconscious movements—things like breathing and blinking and coordination. By interpreting information gathered from the eyes and the ears, it allows us to keep our form and balance and move our muscles exactly when and how we want to move them. Like the cerebrum, the cerebellum is divided into left and right hemispheres and has an irregularly shaped surface.

The last of the three main brain divisions is the brain stem, which connects the cerebrum to the spinal cord. About 3 inches (7.6 centimeters) long, the width of a carrot, and shaped like a funnel, it sticks out from the inferior end of the cerebrum much like the stalk of a plant might protrude from a flower. The brain stem has four major parts: the medulla oblongata, the pons, the midbrain, and the diencephalon.

The medulla oblongata is at the most inferior end of the brain stem and is continuous with the spinal cord. It houses nerve centers that control the body's breathing, heart rate, blood pressure, swallowing, and other important functions. Above the medulla oblongata is the pons. The bulbous, rounded pons has millions of microscopic, thread-like nerve fibers. The smallest part of the brain stem is the midbrain. The midbrain rests just above the pons and helps control eye movement and hearing. Finally, at the top of the brain stem, sandwiched between the midbrain and the cerebrum, is the diencephalon. The various parts of the diencephalon, like the thalamus, hypothalamus, and epithalamus, regulate internal

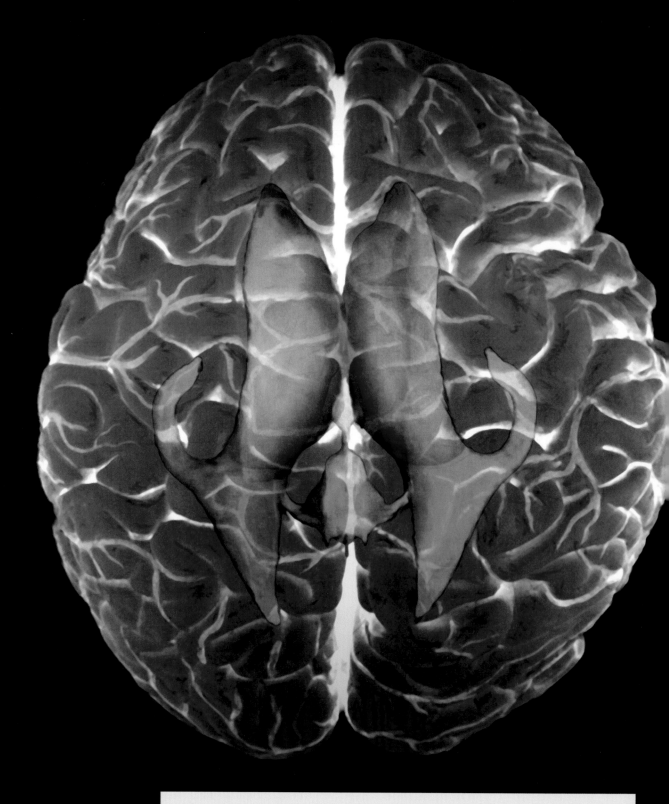

The hollow cavities in the brain that fill with cerebrospinal fluid are called ventricles (shown in brown in this MRI scan).

body conditions like temperature and hunger. They also receive sensory nerve impulses, or sensations, from the rest of the body and relay them to the cerebrum.

THE BRAIN'S FOUR VENTRICLES

Ventricles are cavities or chambers inside the brain that produce and circulate cerebral spinal fluid. The brain has four ventricles. Two of the ventricles, one in each of the cerebral hemispheres, are referred to as lateral ventricles. The other two are known as the third and fourth ventricles. The third ventricle is located in the diencephalon. The fourth ventricle is below the third ventricle. Most CSF is produced in the two lateral ventricles by a structure called the choroid plexus. From there, it flows into the third ventricle, where it is joined by more CSF. It then continues on to the fourth ventricle through a narrow tunnel called the cerebral aqueduct. Once in the fourth ventricle it combines with the CSF produced there. Finally, most of the CSF leaves the ventricular system through holes in the fourth ventricle and enters the subarachnoid space—the space between the arachnoid and the pia mater. From the subarachnoid space the CSF spreads out to bathe the entire surface of the brain and the spinal cord. CSF is constantly produced by the ventricles and, at the same time, drained back into the blood stream through venous sinuses. In the healthy human body, CSF is constantly circulating at all times.

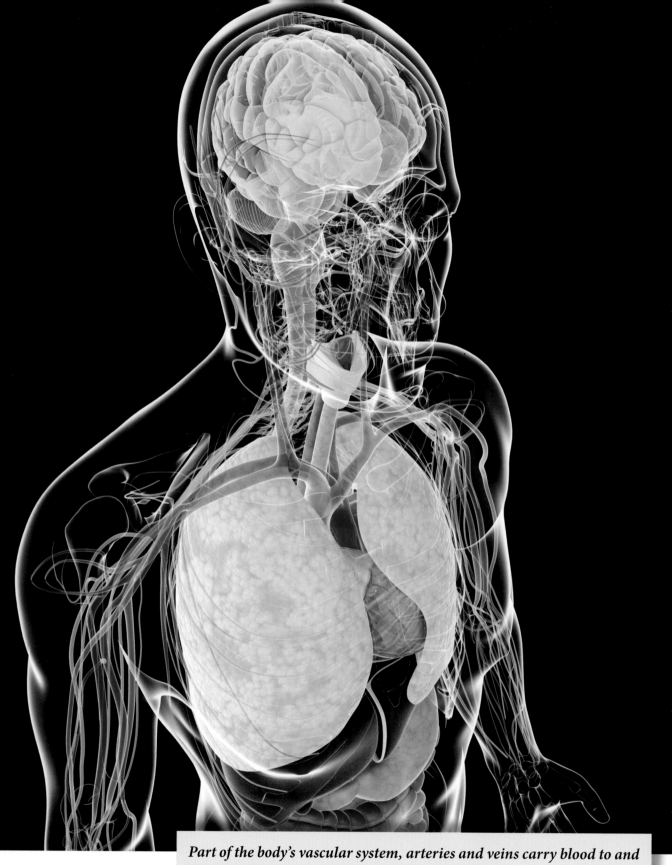

Part of the body's vascular system, arteries and veins carry blood to and from the brain, heart, lungs, and other body parts.

THE VASCULAR SYSTEM: BRINGING BLOOD TO THE BRAIN

The brain, more than any other organ in the human body, needs blood—and the oxygen and nutrients that are in it—to survive. Without oxygen, brain cells would starve and die in just a few minutes. To ensure that the brain doesn't run out of oxygen, the heart does everything and anything to supply it with sufficient amounts of blood. In fact, if necessary, the heart will deliver blood to the brain at the expense of any other organ in the body.

Arteries and veins are part of the body's vascular system. Arteries carry oxygen-rich blood from the heart to the brain, while veins circulate oxygen-poor blood back to the heart. The heart then pumps the venous blood out to the lungs—where the exchange of oxygen-poor blood for highly oxygenated blood occurs—before redirecting it to all other body parts, including the brain.

CHAPTER TWO

THE BRAIN'S PARTNER: THE SPINAL CORD

T he brain cannot work alone. It works in tandem with the spinal cord. Among other things, this long, narrow, white cable of nerves acts as a sort of message delivery system to the brain. The brain sends signals and other information to the rest of the body through the spinal cord. And in turn the body uses the spinal cord to send messages back to the brain.

The superior, or top, end of the spinal cord meets the base of the brain at the brain stem. The inferior end is located about two-thirds of the way down the spinal column. The spinal column is what most of us know as the "backbone." The bony spinal column surrounds the spinal cord like a sheath and helps protect it from injury.

The spinal cord transmits messages bidirectionally between the brain and the rest of the body.

THE BODY'S MEANS OF SUPPORT: THE SPINAL COLUMN

To understand the spinal cord, it helps to know a little about the spinal column. The spinal column, which anatomists also refer to as the vertebral column, is the body's main means of support. The superior end of the spinal column supports the skull, while the bottom links up with the pelvis (the hips). For the most part, it's flexible, allowing a person to bend over, for example, but it's also quite strong.

The spinal column is made up of thirty-three separate bones called vertebrae. Anatomists like to divide these bones into five distinct spinal groups: the cervical spine, the thoracic spine, the lumbar spine, the sacral spine, and the coccyx. The cervical spine is what most people know as the neck. It consists of the first seven vertebrae, which, for identification purposes, are often numbered C1 through C7. C1 is at the very superior end of the spinal column and supports the skull.

Directly below the cervical spine is the thoracic spine. The thoracic spine is essentially the upper back and includes twelve thoracic vertebrae, numbered T1 through T12. The thoracic region coincides with the ribs. Below the thoracic spine are the five vertebrae of the lumbar spine (L1 through L5), or lower back. The muscles near the lumbar spine are often injured by people who lift heavy objects. In adult humans, the spinal cord's inferior end, called the conus medullaris, is between L1 and L2. Next comes the sacral spine, which consists of five vertebrae (S1 through S5) fused together to

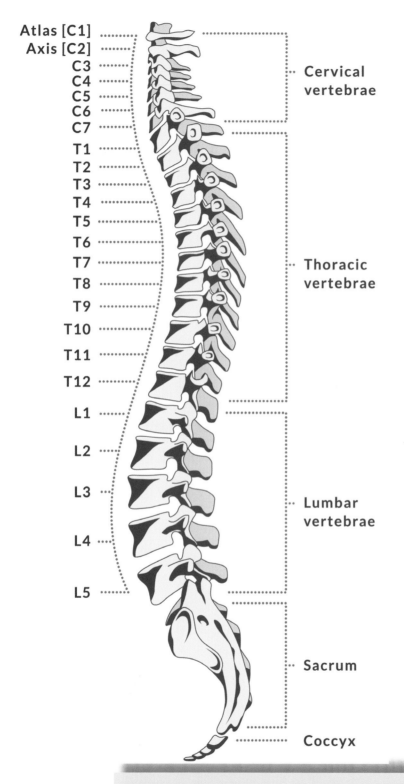

Atlas [C1]
Axis [C2]
C3
C4
C5
C6
C7
T1
T2
T3
T4
T5
T6
T7
T8
T9
T10
T11
T12
L1
L2
L3
L4
L5

Cervical vertebrae

Thoracic vertebrae

Lumbar vertebrae

Sacrum

Coccyx

form one plate-like bone known as the sacrum. The sacrum can be felt as the rigid bone on the back of your pelvis.

The last three to five vertebrae (the number varies from person to person) of the spinal column are also fused together into one curvy bone. This bone is called the coccyx, or tailbone. If you're reclined on a sofa as you read this you're probably resting on your coccyx.

Each vertebra is separated from those above and below it by fluid-filled cushions of sturdy elastic cartilage called intervertebral discs. The discs serve as built-in shock absorbers for the spine. Their elasticity also permits the spine to move.

The vertebrae of the spinal column are divided into five groups: cervical spine, thoracic spine, lumbar spine, sacral spine, and coccyx.

Without them, our backs would be stiff and unmovable like a metal pole. Spinal disc injuries from heavy lifting or over-twisting of the back are very common. However, it is better to slip a disc than it is to harm what's hidden inside it.

PIPELINE OF NERVES: THE SPINAL CORD

The average length of the spinal cord in the adult man is 45 centimeters (17.7 inches). In adult women it tends to be a little bit shorter—about 42 centimeters (16.5 inches). It's anywhere from 6 to 12 millimeters (.2–.4 inches) wide depending on where you measure it, but in general, the farther down the spinal column it goes, the narrower it gets.

The spinal cord serves as the central pipeline for 31 different pairs of spinal nerves (eight cervical, twelve thoracic, five lumbar, five sacral, and one coccygeal). The spinal nerves act like conductors for information traveling between the spinal cord and the rest of the body. The anatomy is extremely complex. Protruding from the spinal cord are spinal roots. The spinal roots attach to spinal nerves. The spinal nerves then split into ventral and dorsal (front and back) rami. Finally, the rami, which contain thread-like nervous fibers, branch out to the rest of the body. To simplify, imagine the spinal nerves to be two rows of thirty-one trees planted along a strip of ground. The strip of ground is the spinal cord, the tree trunks are the spinal nerves, and the tree branches are the rami. The rami reach far and wide to every corner of the human body, including the legs, the arms, the hands, and the feet.

THE BRAIN AND ANESTHESIA

The effective treatment of illness often requires surgery, and surgery was simply not practical before the appearance of drugs to relieve pain. Before the middle of the nineteenth century, surgery was seen only as a last resort and an act of desperation that killed as many patients as it cured. Doctors who recorded their impressions of surgery before painkillers describe scenes of screaming reminiscent of the medieval torture chamber. And yet many people, including some doctors, were not entirely comfortable with efforts to alleviate pain. Some believed that pain was the Lord's punishment for the wicked and a trial for the righteous. In the late sixteenth century, a woman in Edinburgh, Scotland, was buried alive for seeking relief from the pain of childbirth from another woman accused of witchcraft.

Drugs like laudanum, a mixture of opium and alcohol, had been around for a long time. In 1800, English chemist Humphrey Davy (1778–1829) suggested the use of nitrous oxide as a painkiller. In 1803, Friedrich Wilhelm Sertürner (1783–1841) isolated crystals of morphine from crude opium, but it could not be administered effectively until the invention of the syringe in the 1850s. In 1897, Felix Hoffmann (1868–1946), working for the German firm Bayer, developed the compound acetylsalicylic acid, which was marketed as a painkiller under the trade name Aspirin. All of these substances, however, had drawbacks. They were either not strong enough for surgical procedures, difficult to administer in the right doses, or they induced unpleasant side effects.

Ether, a compound made from sulfuric acid and alcohol, was discovered by the Spanish chemist Raymundus Lullius (1232–1315) in 1275, but it was centuries before its anesthetic properties were recognized. The first use of ether as a surgical anesthetic was by the American surgeon Dr. Crawford Williams Long (1815–1878) on March 30, 1842, when he removed two tumors from the neck of a patient. Dr. Long performed eight more operations using ether in the following years, but he did not publish his results until 1849. For this reason, the credit for the first use of ether as an anesthetic has gone to another American, Dr. William Thomas Green Morton (1819–1868).

Dr. Morton was a dentist, and early in 1846 he began to experiment with ether at his home in West Needham, Massachusetts, dosing not only small animals but himself. In September of that year, in his Boston office, he used ether to painlessly extract a tooth from a patient. Local press reports of his success brought Morton to the attention of Dr. John Collins Warren, senior surgeon at Massachusetts General Hospital. On the morning of October 16, 1846, Dr. Morton brought his ether apparatus to Dr. Warren's operating theater at Mass General and anesthetized Edward Gilbert Abbott, a twenty-year-old man with a tumor in his neck. "Your patient is ready, sir," said Dr. Morton, and Dr. Warren then successfully removed the tumor. After the procedure, Dr. Warren turned to the prestigious group of doctors in the gallery and said, "Gentlemen, this is no humbug." Painless surgery had arrived. Shortly after the demonstration, Oliver Wendell Holmes (1809–1894), a professor of anatomy soon to become dean of Harvard Medical School, wrote to Morton and suggested the name "anesthesia" for the state of unconsciousness induced by ether.

Almost immediately afterward, the Scottish physician James Young Simpson (1811–1870) tried to substitute chloroform for ether because of ether's disagreeable odor. In the long term he was not successful because chloroform is more volatile and difficult to handle safely, but he did perform a number of painless procedures using chloroform, most of them attempts to alleviate the pain of childbirth. Here he encountered religious prejudice against the use of anesthetics during childbirth. But in 1853, Queen Victoria appointed Simpson her personal physician and chose to be anesthetized for the births of her seventh and eighth children. As a result, the prejudice against anesthetics quickly fell away, and in upper- and middle-class families painless childbirth became quite common.

With the exception of the very first spinal nerve, C1, spinal nerves exit the spinal column between vertebrae. For example, spinal nerve C2 exits the spinal cord between vertebrae C1 and C2, and spinal nerve C8 exits between vertebrae C7 and T1. C1, the oddball, exits between the C1 vertebra, which is also known as the atlas (the word "atlas" comes from hero of Greek mythology who held the world on his shoulders), and the occipital bone of the skull, which rests on top of the atlas. The thoracic, lumbar, and sacral nerves of the spinal cord exit the spinal column below the vertebrae by the same number. So spinal nerve L1, for example, exits between the L1 and L2 vertebrae. And spinal nerve S1 exits between the S1 and S2 vertebrae.

The spinal cord is much shorter than the spinal column, so spinal nerves near the inferior end of the cord, especially the lumbar and sacral nerves, must travel down the column for a ways before they can exit between vertebrae. Picture spinal nerve S2, for instance. It enters the spinal column at about the same level as the L1 vertebrae but exits between the S2 and S3 vertebrae. So it has to travel down the column just to get out. As a result, there is a tail-like collection of nerves near the inferior end of the spinal column that anatomists call the cauda equina. *Cauda equina* is Latin for "horse's tail."

THE SPINAL CORD'S MENINGES

Like the brain, the spinal cord is protected by three layers of meninges—the dura mater, the arachnoid, and the pia mater—

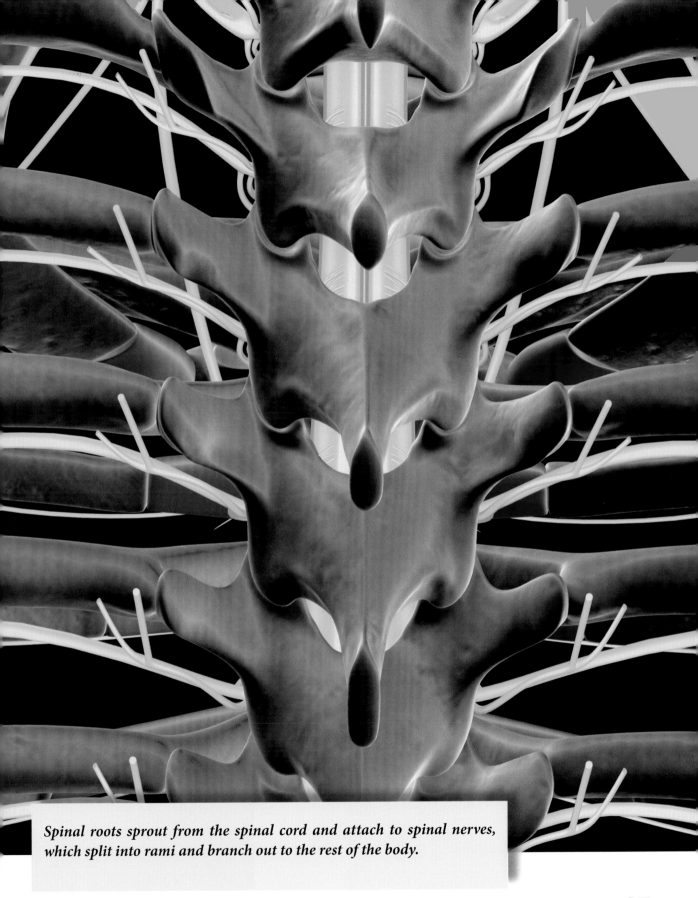

Spinal roots sprout from the spinal cord and attach to spinal nerves, which split into rami and branch out to the rest of the body.

and circulating cerebral spinal fluid. The meninges travel most of the length of the spinal column, continuing far past the inferior end of the spinal cord in the lumbar area to form a bag-like "meningeal sac" in the sacral area. Doctors often "tap" this sac to collect and test samples of the cerebral spinal fluid inside it to look for certain diseases.

Another major guard against spinal cord injury is, not surprisingly, the vertebrae of the spinal column. Vertebrae come in all different sizes, but their basic structure is the same. The main part of the bone is called the vertebral body. It makes the spinal column strong. Attached to the vertebral body is the vertebral arch, which surrounds and protects the spinal cord like a personal bodyguard. Protruding from the vertebral arch are various fin-like "processes." The processes do things like attach to back muscles, restrict potentially dangerous movements, and prevent vertebral discs from slipping.

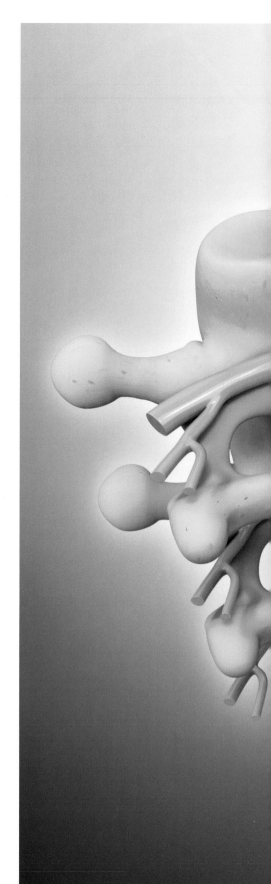

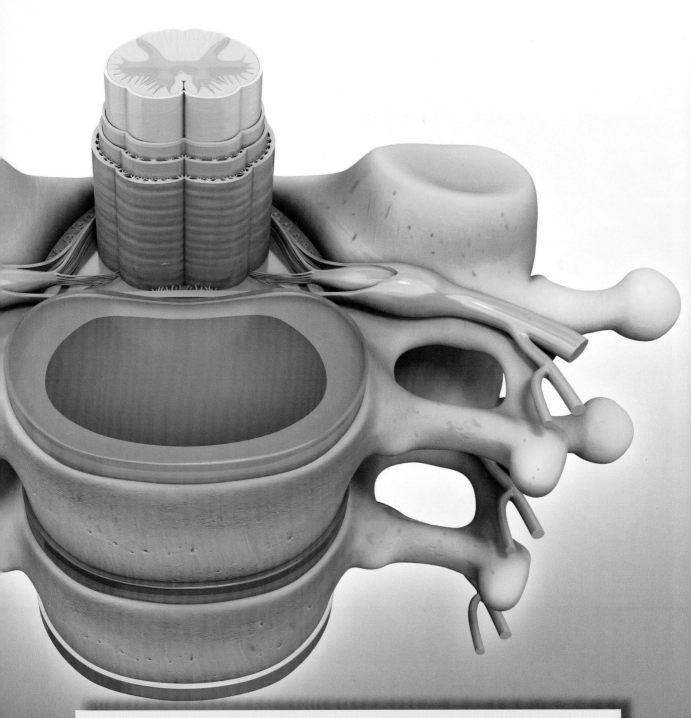

Three layers of meninges protect the spinal cord, as shown in this cross-section: dura mater, arachnoid, and pia mater. Cerebral spinal fluid serves as protection, too.

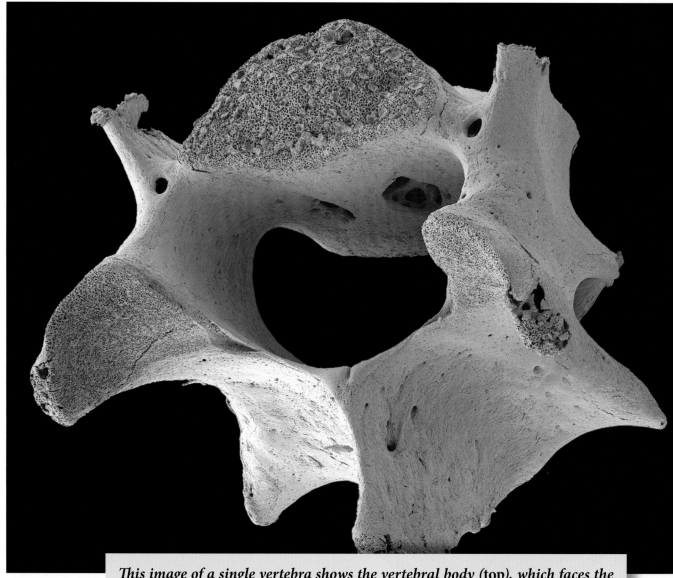

This image of a single vertebra shows the vertebral body (top), which faces the chest, and vertebral arch (bottom), which faces the back. The hole in the center is called the vertebral foramen, and the spinal cord runs through it.

CHAPTER THREE

EMOTION, THINKING, AND THE BRAIN

The anatomy and functions of the brain and spinal cord are pretty well understood by scientists, who have been studying them for quite some time. However, there is more to these two powerhouses of the body: they also play a big part in the emotions that we experience. How can we study our feelings of anger, fear, happiness, and sadness using science? Is such a thing even possible? Until recently, many researchers considered emotions to be so different from person to person that they thought scientific studies of the subject would be useless and inaccurate. How could you ever claim love, for instance, is an identical experience from one person to the next? As a result, relatively little serious research was ever conducted.

Today, however, the mood has changed, and high-tech brain-scanning tools are now being used to figure out exactly what parts of the brain play the biggest role in the emotional world. By studying the unique pathways that different emotions

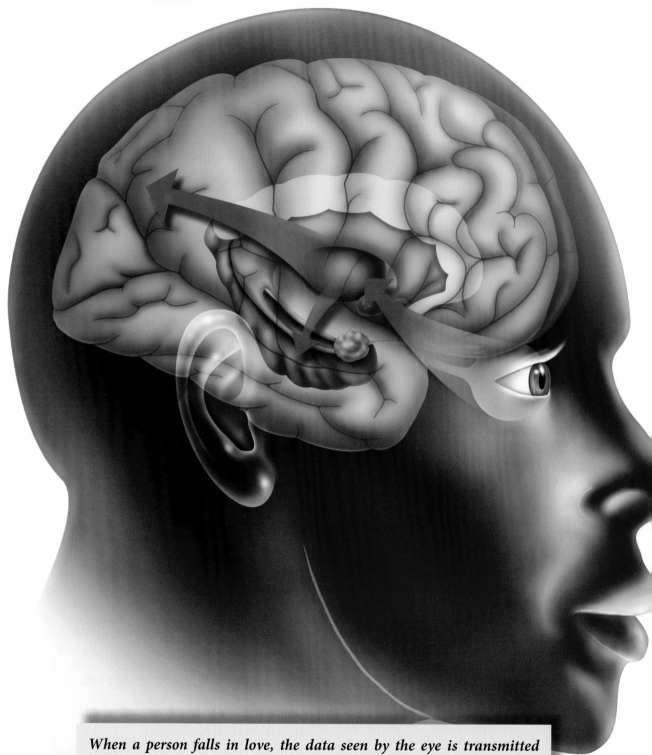

When a person falls in love, the data seen by the eye is transmitted to the thalamus and the visual cortex. The thalamus sends data to the hippocampus, and the person is able to compare the vision with memories he or she has stored. This is the first of three stages.

follow through the brain, scientists have discovered that no one part of the brain is entirely responsible for how we experience those emotions. Emotions are processed by almost every area of the brain, they say. Our bodies respond to life's emotional experiences in many different ways, both physically and mentally, and our personal responses to those experiences are a result of everything coming together in the brain.

Interestingly, using these scanning techniques, scientists now know why emotions can affect a person's ability to think. When we experience extreme emotions, like an intense feeling of love for someone close to us, the flurry of neural activity that results affects the brain like a severe internal electrical storm. The interference prevents the brain from interpreting new information—from thinking.

THE EMOTIONAL BRAIN: THE LIMBIC SYSTEM

While many areas of the brain play a role in our emotions, the limbic system is definitely the most important. In fact, the limbic system is so important in producing emotions that it's often referred to as the "emotional brain."

Human emotions can result from a specific thought or from a message delivered to the brain from sensory organs (triggered by something you see, smell, or hear). Both situations create nerve impulses that travel to the limbic system. There, depending on what the message or thought is, the impulses kick different parts of the limbic system into gear. The system, in turn, produces emotions. Good, bad, pleasant, unpleasant—it all depends on the information the limbic system receives.

The limbic system is made up of two main parts: the cortical region and the subcortical region. Within the cortical region is the hippocampus. One of the things the hippocampus influences is the release of a hormone from the body's adrenal gland that affects moods and behaviors. For example, in times of stress—like when you're worried about a tough test that is coming up—this natural substance, known as corticosteroid hormone, enters your blood stream.

In the subcortical region three parts in particular play major roles in emotions. One part is the septum, also known as the brain's "pleasure center." This is where the brain recognizes certain sensations as pleasurable.

The subcortical region's amygdala, on the other hand, regulates emotions like fear, arousal, and anger. The amygdala is located in the temporal lobe of the brain. One of the main jobs of the amygdala is to create connections between stimuli and their emotional value (whether a particular stimulus is good or bad). This occurs through memories, which almost always include an emotional aspect. If deep in your mind you remember that a certain incident made you sad, for instance, the next time a similar incident occurs your brain will tell you to be sad again. In scientific experiments, wild animals with damaged amygdalas lose their fear of potentially dangerous predators and humans.

The last main part of the subcortical region of the limbic system is called the hypothalamus. "Hypothalamus" means

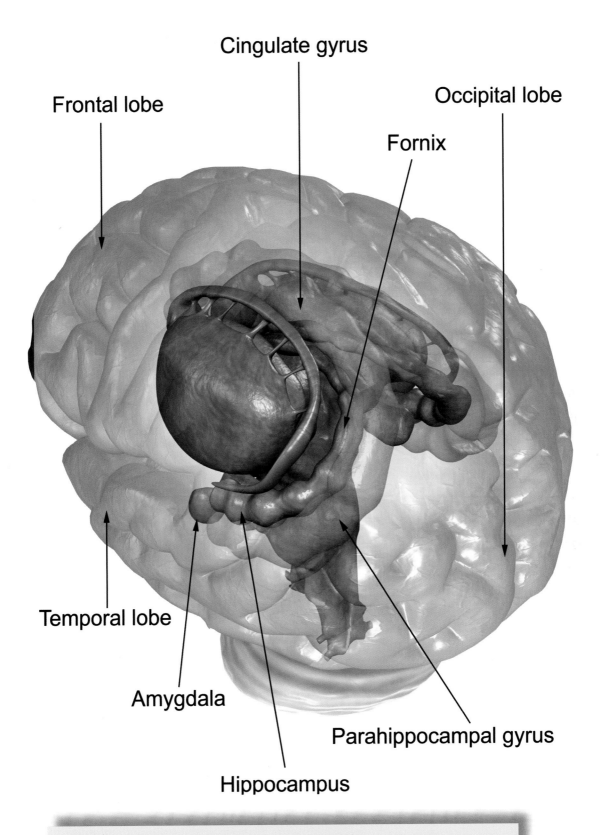

Cingulate gyrus

Frontal lobe

Occipital lobe

Fornix

Temporal lobe

Amygdala

Parahippocampal gyrus

Hippocampus

The limbic system is a loosely connected network of structures. Emotion, memory, and motivation all are regulated by the limbic system.

RECOGNIZING FACIAL EXPRESSIONS

Thanks to neuroscientists at the University of Iowa, we now know that the right prefrontal cortex, a region at the front of the brain's right hemisphere, is the part of the brain that allows us to recognize and interpret the facial expressions of other people. During a rare surgical operation in which the scientists inserted special depth electrodes into their patient's brain while he was awake, they were able to see that neurons in the right prefrontal cortex were activated as he was shown photographs of strangers with unique facial expressions and interpreted those emotions. So, next time you see someone frown and you know that he's sad, or you watch a person smile and you're sure that she's happy, thank your brain—the right prefrontal cortex of your brain, that is.

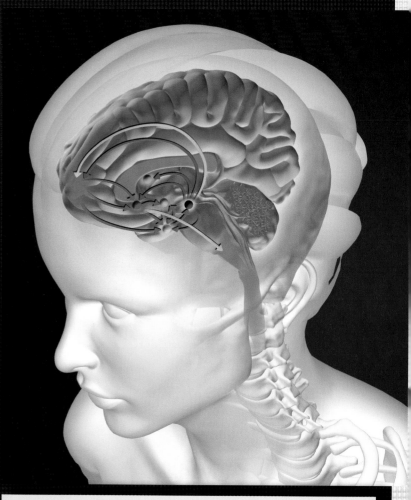

Clues to recognizing facial expressions are processed in the brain's right prefrontal cortex.

"under the thalamus," and that's exactly where it's located—at the base of the diencephalon, inferior to the thalamus. The hypothalamus does a lot of things, but when it comes to emotions, it primarily regulates anger, pain, sex, pleasure, and survival instincts like the desire for food and water. An animal with a damaged hypothalamus might even forget to eat and starve to death. The hypothalamus also regulates the pituitary gland, which hangs from the hypothalamus and

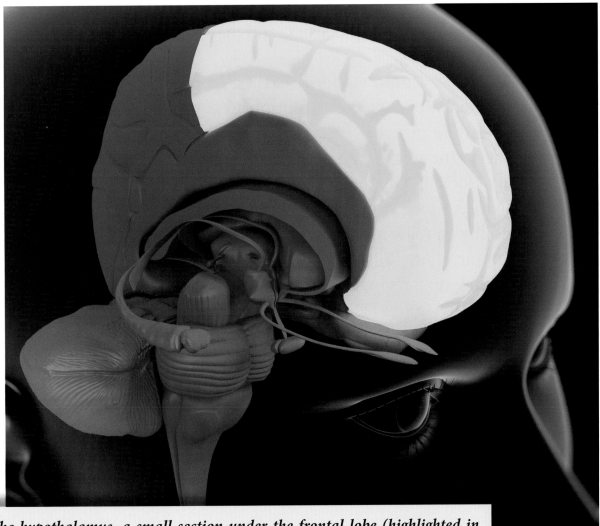

The hypothalamus, a small section under the frontal lobe (highlighted in yellow), regulates the body's basic biological needs, such as hunger and temperature control.

secretes several hormones that control important bodily functions.

HOW THE BRAIN PROCESSES THINKING AND MEMORY

Much like the anatomy of emotions, thinking and memory involve extremely complex brain activities. Scientists are still deciphering how thoughts work, and they're learning new things every day.

When we think, we form, create, or process something in our mind. We ponder the solution to a problem, we imagine ourselves in a different place, or we remember something from long ago. One part of the brain known to play a role in thought is the association cortex of the cerebrum, in the frontal lobes. The brain's association areas give us our intellectual abilities, our ability to reason and to make plans, and our language and communication skills. They also influence how smart we are, what kind of personality we have, and our decision-making abilities. They allow us to imagine what might happen should we do something—before we actually do it. They permit us to understand why someone might feel a particular way and what his or her reasons are for doing certain things. Scientists have found that people with damaged frontal lobes lose the ability to think and reason in these ways. They often act in strange, socially unacceptable ways, and their emotional reactions to certain situations become very unpredictable.

The way thought works is complex. Information gathered from the senses enters the association cortex, is interpreted and processed, and is combined—or associated—with information

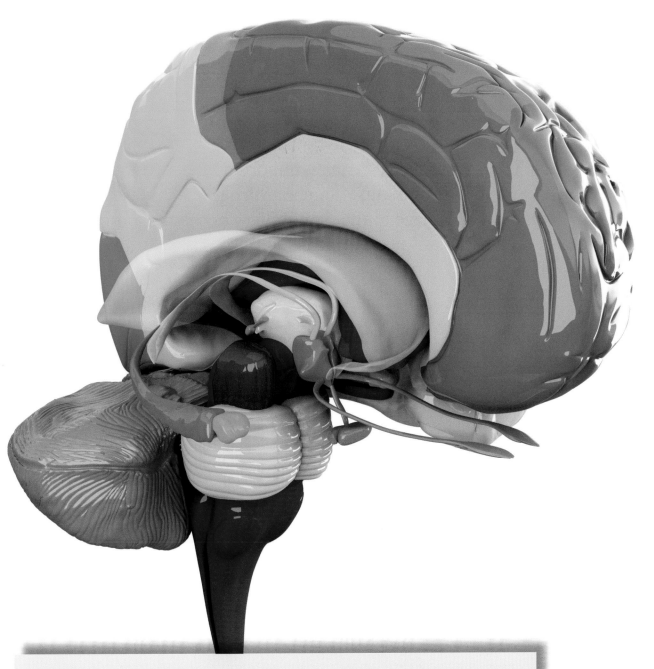

Located in the frontal lobes, the association cortex is responsible for the processing and conversion of input to behavior generation.

39

that is already stored in memory. The more abstract and difficult the ideas or subjects the brain tries to process, the more complex that processing becomes. Learning and memory take place primarily in the hippocampus, which, as mentioned above, is a part of the limbic system. Scientists believe the hippocampus acts like a storage center for memories and helps people to form new memories.

Another region of the brain involved in memory is the mammillary bodies of the hypothalamus. The mammillary bodies, which are reflex centers important for the sense of smell, sprout like miniature antennae from the floor of the hypothalamus. Damage to the mammillary bodies can result in severe memory loss—a condition called Korsakov's syndrome.

CHAPTER FOUR

TRANSMITTING MESSAGES: THE NERVOUS SYSTEM

The brain and spinal cord team up with the body's countless nerves and receptors to form the nervous system. The human nervous system allows the body to send messages to and receive messages from all its parts. Because of the nervous system, the body is able to respond to stimuli from the outside world, such as light, sound, and heat. It also permits the body to react to changes inside it, like decreasing oxygen levels, for example.

The nervous system communicates with the rest of the body by sending rapid electrical impulses to specific body parts. In order to know what signals to send, the nervous system does three things. First, it relies on millions of tiny sensory receptors to sense changes occurring both inside and outside of the body. Second, it takes the information gathered by the receptors, called sensory input, figures out what that information means, and decides what to do about it. Finally, with a decision

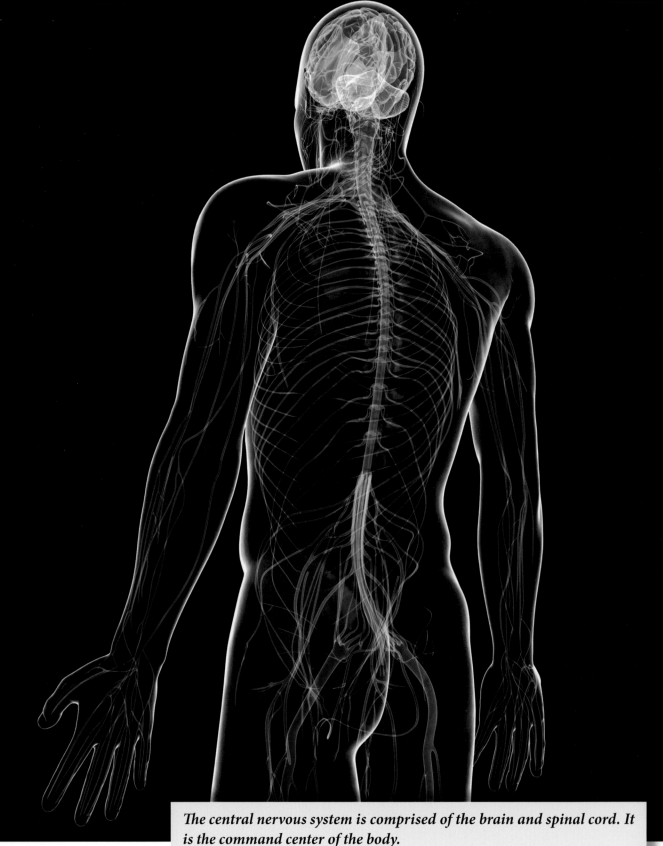

The central nervous system is comprised of the brain and spinal cord. It is the command center of the body.

in hand, the nervous system responds to the sensory input with motor output—a reaction. Two examples of motor output are the movement of a muscle and the secretion of sweat or saliva from glands.

PARTS OF THE NERVOUS SYSTEM

There are two major parts to the human nervous system: the central nervous system and the peripheral nervous system. The central nervous system, or CNS, consists of the brain and the spinal cord. Together, the brain and the spinal cord serve as the nervous system's command station. When sensory input arrives at the CNS, the brain and spinal cord figure out exactly what it means. Then, almost instantaneously, they fire orders out to the body parts that need to be mobilized.

Everything outside of the central nervous system is known as the peripheral nervous system, or PNS. The PNS includes all the nerves that leave the brain and spinal cord and travel to various parts of the body. The nerves carrying information in the form of nerve impulses to and from the brain are called cranial nerves. Those that carry nerve impulses to and from the spine are called spinal nerves. The peripheral nervous system's main job is to send information gathered from the body's sensory receptors as quickly as possible to the central nervous system. Then, once the CNS has interpreted that information, the PNS instantly relays specific orders back out to the body.

There are two main parts to the peripheral nervous system. The first part is the sensory division. The sensory division is like the body's incoming mail server. It collects impulses from sensory receptors in places like the skin, muscles, and organs, and carries those impulses through nerves to the central nervous system.

The second main part of the peripheral nervous system is the motor division. The motor division has the opposite job of the sensory division. It collects the outgoing messages from the central nervous system and delivers them to the appropriate body organs, effectively telling them exactly what to do.

The motor division itself can be divided into two parts: the autonomic nervous system and the somatic nervous system. The autonomic nervous system is responsible for

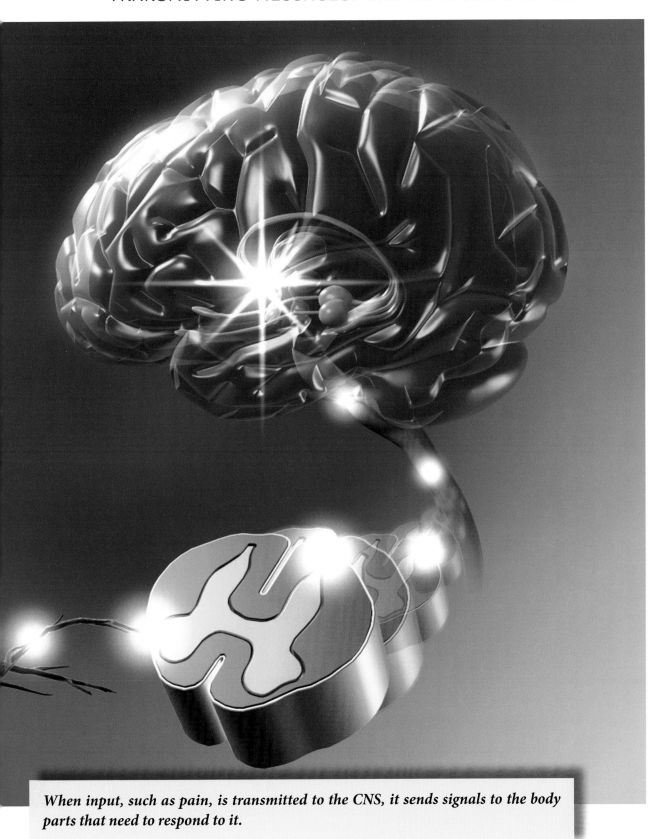

When input, such as pain, is transmitted to the CNS, it sends signals to the body parts that need to respond to it.

controlling automatic body functions—those activities of the body we have no conscious control over, like the everyday beating of the heart. The autonomic nervous system often kicks in when we experience stressful things like severe injury, blood loss, or fright. Not surprisingly, the autonomic nervous system is also known as

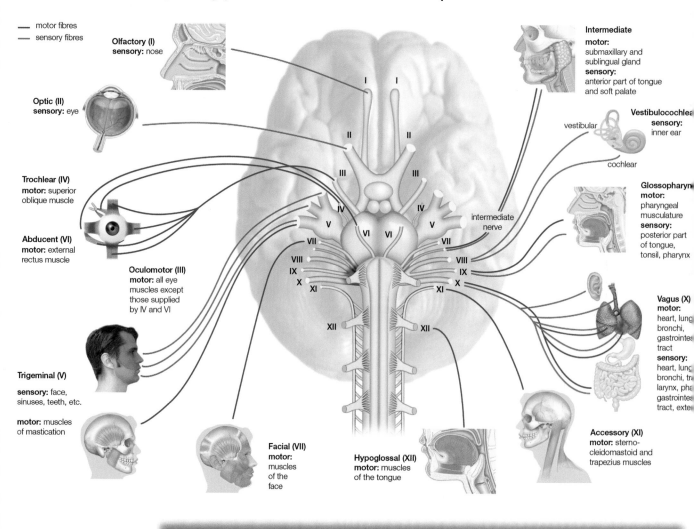

This illustration shows the pathways from the cranial nerves to the body.

the involuntary nervous system. The somatic nervous system, on the other hand, is responsible for our voluntary movements—those muscle movements we consciously decide we would like to make. Another name for the somatic nervous system is the voluntary nervous system.

REFLEXES: THE BODY'S RESPONSE TO STIMULUS

A reflex is an automatic nervous system response to stimulus. Reflexes occur whether we want them to or not. We are born with them—our bodies are ready to use them from the very second we come into the world. Most reflexes are very important for everyday functioning. We use them all the time. For example, we have reflexes for swallowing and blinking. Some reflexes can be controlled. For instance, we have reflexes that make us want to urinate, but we can usually prevent ourselves from urinating until we find a bathroom.

There are two types of reflexes: autonomic reflexes and somatic reflexes. Autonomic reflexes control things like digestion, urination, sweating, and blood pressure. Somatic reflexes are reflexes that control skeletal muscles. For example, when you touch your tongue to a cup of scorching hot water, a somatic reflex makes you quickly pull away—hopefully before you burn yourself. The path a reflex follows through the nervous system is called a reflex arc.

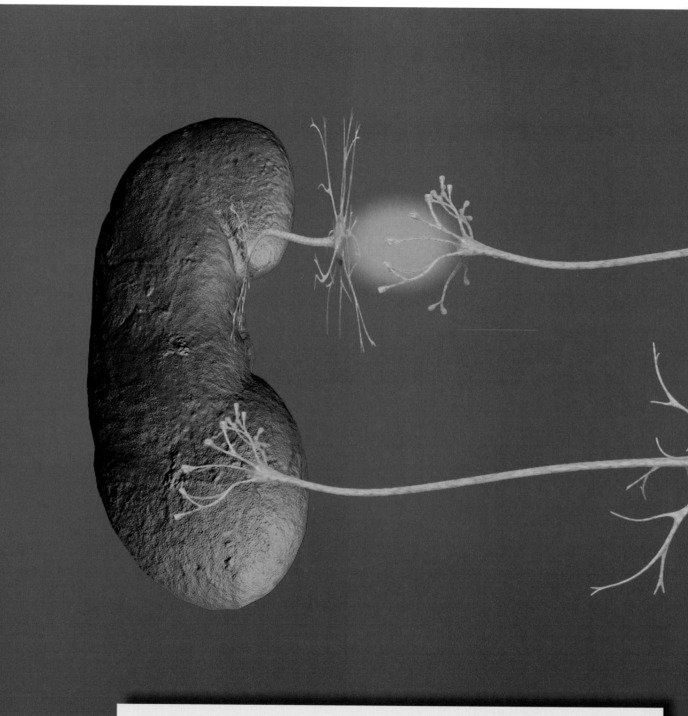

This illustration compares the somatic and autonomic nervous systems. The somatic nervous system controls the skeletal muscles after the brain has given its orders in response to environmental stimuli. The autonomic nervous system is responsible for keeping the body running smoothly without conscious effort.

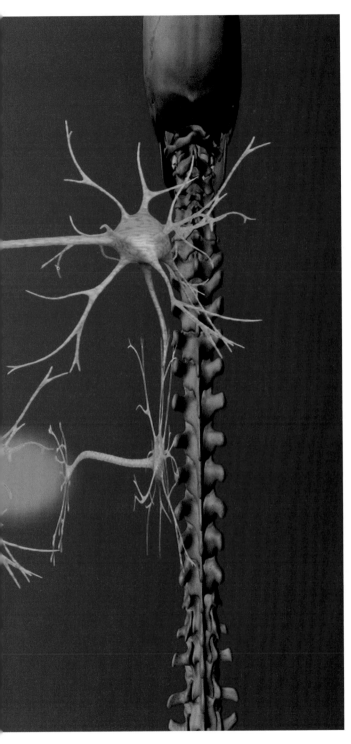

THE CELLS OF THE NERVOUS SYSTEM

The nervous system is made of two types of cells. Nerve cells, known as neurons, are cells of the nervous system that transmit messages throughout the body. Neurons consist of nerve bodies, which receive stimuli, and thread-like nerve processes—or axons—which carry the stimuli to other neurons and to organs. Neurons respond to stimuli with an electrical discharge called a nerve impulse from a receptor and then conduct that nerve impulse along a chain of neurons all the way to the brain.

Neurons are very close to one another, but they do not touch. Instead, there's a space between each one

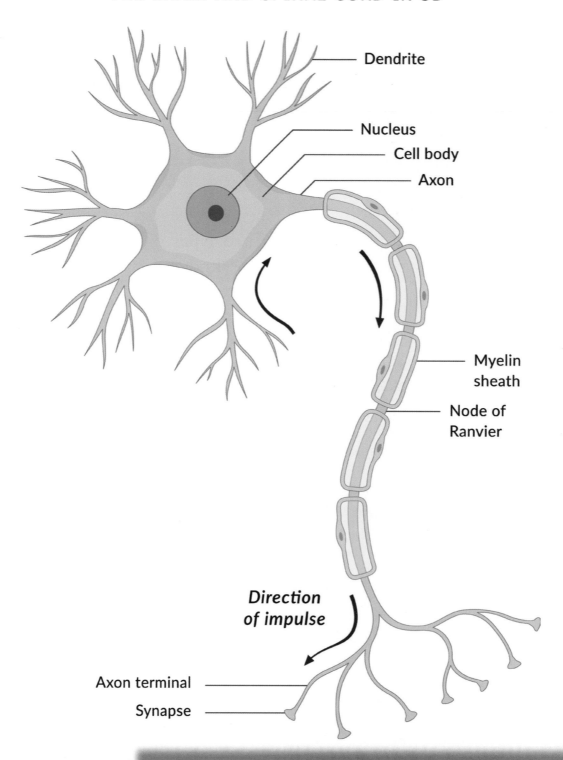

Dendrite

Nucleus

Cell body

Axon

Myelin sheath

Node of Ranvier

Direction of impulse

Axon terminal

Synapse

Neurons receive stimuli and respond with an electrical discharge called a nerve impulse.

called a synaptic cleft through which information is transmitted by means of chemicals known as neurotransmitters. Information is passed through one neuron, transmitted through a synaptic cleft, and then picked up by the next neuron, and then the process is repeated. The entire process is called a synapse.

The second type of cells, glial cells, are so-called supporting cells. They help the neurons do their job. For instance, some glial cells lay down a substance called myelin (a fat layer) that allows the electrical impulse to travel faster. Other glial cells defend neurons by attacking bacteria and dangerous foreign substances. There are far more glial cells in the nervous system than there are neurons, but that should be expected. One can never have too many helpers, after all.

GRAY MATTER AND WHITE MATTER

If you were to take a knife and carve a slice out of the brain, the inside surface of the resulting sliver of nervous tissue would be colored both white and gray. The white, centrally located areas are known as white matter. The gray areas near the outside, in the cortex, are called gray matter and consist of neuronal cell bodies. White matter is made of axons, the thread-like fibers that branch away from the neuronal cell bodies and conduct nerve impulses. The axons get their white color from myelin, a fatty material that forms a protective and insulating sheath around them.

Like the brain, the spinal cord is also composed of gray matter and white matter. Snip it in two and the gray and white

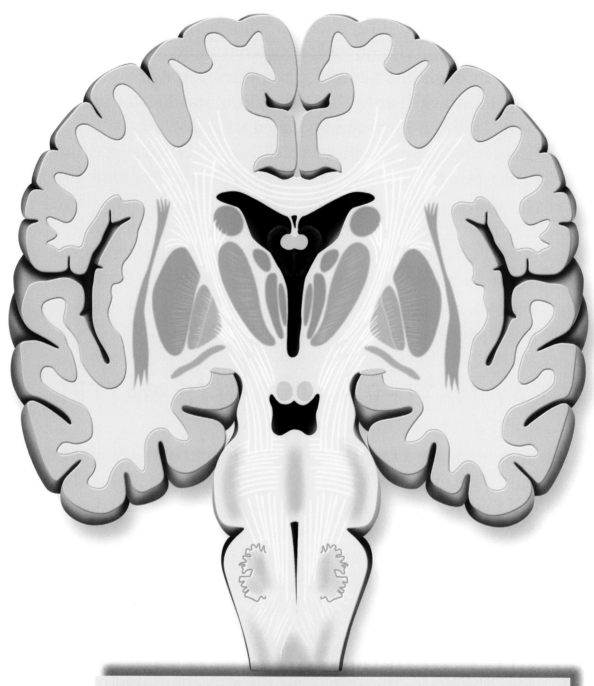

This frontal cutaway view of the brain highlights the white matter and gray matter of the brain's nervous tissue.

sections can be seen by the naked eye. The outer part of the cord is made of white matter, while the central part—shaped like an H—is made of gray matter. Again, spinal cord white matter consists of axons that carry signals to and from the brain. And spinal cord gray matter consists of neuronal cell bodies.

GLOSSARY

AUTONOMIC NERVOUS SYSTEM The body system responsible for controlling automatic body functions, like breathing and swallowing.

AXON Finger-like strand of nerve tissue that carries information to neurons and to organs.

CENTRAL NERVOUS SYSTEM The part of the nervous system that includes the brain and the spinal cord.

CEREBRAL SPINAL FLUID (CSF) A clear, water-like substance that circulates within the subarachnoid space of the brain and the spinal cord.

EMOTIONS Human feelings such as happiness, sadness, anger, and fear.

GRAY MATTER Gray regions of the brain and spinal cord consisting of neuronal cell bodies.

LIMBIC SYSTEM A brain-based system that scientists believe is important for processing emotions.

MEMBRANE A thin layer of body tissue.

MENINGES Layers of tissue that protect the brain and the spinal cord.

MOTOR OUTPUT The body's reaction to stimulus.

NERVE FIBER Thread-like strand of nerves that can transmit information.

NERVE IMPULSE An electrical discharge from a neuron that is conducted to the brain.

NERVOUS SYSTEM The body system that includes the brain, the spinal cord, nerves, and receptors, and which controls both voluntary and involuntary actions.

PERIPHERAL NERVOUS SYSTEM The part of the nervous system outside of the brain and the spinal cord.

RECEPTOR A cell or group of cells that senses stimuli from inside or outside of the body.

REFLEX An automatic nervous system response to stimulus.

SENSORY INPUT Information gathered by body receptors and transmitted to the central nervous system.

SOMATIC NERVOUS SYSTEM A body system responsible for voluntary movements.

SYNAPSE A space between two neurons through which information is transmitted.

TISSUE A collection of cells that forms a structural material of the body.

VASCULAR SYSTEM A body system consisting of various channels that circulate blood.

VENTRICLE Chamber inside the brain that produces and circulates cerebral spinal fluid.

VERTEBRAL COLUMN The spinal column, consisting of thirty-three vertebrae and intervertebral discs.

WHITE MATTER White regions of the brain and spinal cord consisting of axons.

FOR MORE INFORMATION

American Academy of Neurology

201 Chicago Avenue

Minneapolis, MN 55415

Website: http://www.aan.com

Founded in 1948, the AAN now represents more than twenty-eight thousand members and is dedicated to promoting the highest quality patient-centered care and enhancing member career satisfaction.

American Medical Association

330 N. Wabash Avenue

Chicago, IL 60611

(800) 621-8335

Website: http://www.ama-assn.org

The American Medical Association promotes the art and science of medicine and the betterment of public health.

Society for Neuroscience

1121 14th Street NW, Suite 1010

Washington DC 20005

(202) 962-4000

Website: http://www.sfn.org

Membership in the Society for Neuroscience brings exceptional value for neuroscience professionals at all career stages, providing a wide range of world-class programs, publications, and services for the field and members across the globe.

WEBSITES

Because of the changing nature of Internet links, Rosen Publishing has developed an online list of websites related to the subject of this book. This site is updated regularly. Please use this link to access this list:

http://www.rosenlinks.com/HB3D/Brain

FOR FURTHER READING

Bouter, Ben, and Iris Bouter. *2,139 Facts About Brains, Psyche, and Nutrition*. Frederick, MD: Publish America, 2014.

Brodal, Per. *The Central Nervous System*. New York, NY: Oxford University Press, 2010.

Carter, Rita. *The Human Brain Book*. New York, NY: DK Publishing, 2014.

Fix, James. *Atlas of the Human Brain and Spinal Cord*. Sudbury, MA: Jones and Barlett, 2008.

Kiernan, John A. and Nagalingam Rajakumar. *The Human Nervous System*. Baltimore, MD: LWW, 2013.

Noback., Charles R. *The Human Nervous System*. CreateSpace Publishing, 2014.

Parker, Steve. *Spinal Cord and Nerves*. Chicago, IL: Heinemann, 2009.

Pinel, John P.J. *A Colorful Introduction to the Anatomy of the Human Brain*. Boston, MA: Pearson, 2007.

Sweeney, Michael S. *Brain: The Complete Mind*. Washington, DC: National Geographic, 2009.

Vanderah, Todd W., and Douglas J. Gould. *Nolte's the Human Brain*. Philadelphia, PA: Elsevier Health Sciences, 2015.

INDEX

INDEX

ABOUT THE AUTHORS

Jack Becker is a science writer and former teacher who lives outside Omaha, Nebraska, with his wife and six children.

Chris Hayhurst is an emergency medical technician, professional author, and journalist with more than a dozen books and hundreds of articles in print. He lives and works in Fort Collins, Colorado.

PHOTO CREDITS